A PRIZE FOR PURRY

Jody found the white kitten
in the pet shop.
They liked each other at once.

She showed her mother,
then watched eagerly
to see what she would say.
Jody's mother smiled.
"Is that the one you want?"
she asked.

"Yes, *please*," cried Jody.

She could feel
the kitten purring,
as if it knew
that it was wanted.

But something seemed to be wrong.
The pet shop lady
was talking to Jody's mother
and pointing to the kitten.
Jody waited anxiously
for her mother to tell her
what was happening.

"Jody," said her mother,
"the shop lady says
that white male kittens
with blue eyes
are often born deaf.
Do you still want him?"

"Of *course* I do!" cried Jody.
"I want him more than ever."

The pet-shop lady opened the cage
and lifted the white kitten out.
"Do you want a box to carry him in?"
she asked Jody.

"No, thanks," smiled Jody.

Jody held her new kitten on her lap
all the way home in the car.

The kitten was purring and purring.
Jody could hear him with her fingers.
"I think I'll call him Purry," she said.

Every day Jody fed Purry
and brushed him and played with him.

He grew bigger...and BIGGER...and BIGGER.
He was a healthy, handsome, happy cat.

At school one day,
Jody's teacher had something special
to tell the class.
First she checked the hearing aids
of the deaf children.

Then she signaled to them
to watch her lips.

"There is going to be a
Children's Pet Show
at the Town Hall next week,"
Mrs. Berry announced.
"There will be prizes
for pet owners,
and prizes for best pets."

Mrs. Berry was still talking,
but Jody's eyes
had left her teacher's face
because her thoughts
had flown away to Purry.
He would *surely* win a prize!

When Jody remembered
to look again, Mrs. Berry
was talking about
drawing pictures.
"I want your picture
to be about your pet," she said.
"If you don't have
a pet, any animal
will do."

Jody liked drawing.
She drew a picture of Purry
asleep with his tongue half out,
dreaming of mice.

She wanted to take
her picture home,
but Mrs. Berry asked
if she could have it.
Of course Jody said "yes."

On the day of the Pet Show,
Jody brushed and combed Purry
and tied a blue bow around his neck.
He looked beautiful.

Everyone had to wait outside the Town Hall
while the pets were being judged.
At last, the doors opened.

Jody and her mother rushed inside.
There were cards on some
of the cages — for first,
second, or third — but *none*
for Purry.

The cat judge came over to Jody.
He was wearing a hearing aid too.
He stooped down
so that Jody could read
his lips and hands.

"I would like to have given
your cat a prize, Jody,
but some people don't understand,
like we do, that being deaf
doesn't really make him different."

21

Jody nodded sadly.
Just then Mrs. Berry touched her arm.

"Come with me, Jody.
I have something to show you,"
she said with a smile.

The wall on the other side
of the hall was covered
with children's drawings.
Right in the middle,
with a card pinned to it,
was Jody's picture of Purry!

"Congratulations, Jody," said Mrs. Berry.
"There are *two* prizes
in the art competition —
a pet food coupon for your cat,
and a paintbox for you.
You and Purry
are *both* winners!"